WARSAW

CHRISTIAN PARMA

WARSAW

Wydawnictwo PARMA® PRESS

Cover photos: Castle Square; Old Town Mermaid; city centre

Title pages: View of Castle Square with the Royal Castle and King Sigismund's Column

Photos: CHRISTIAN PARMA

Text: RENATA GRUNWALD-KOPEĆ

Layout: BOGNA PARMA
Maps: MARIUSZ SZELEREWICZ

Translation: ELŻBIETA KOWALEWSKA
Production: STUDIO PARMA IMAGE, +48 22 / 679 80 53

Publishers: Wydawnictwo PARMA PRESS
03 310 Warszawa, Staniewicka 12
+48 22 / 675 80 07, 675 87 50, 675 77 26
e-mail: wydawnictwo@parmapress.com.pl
http://www.parma press.com.pl

ISBN 83-85743-52-9

© Copyright by **Wydawnictwo** PARMA® PRESS   Warszawa 2000

HISTORICAL FRAMEWORK

Warsaw is one of the youngest European capitals. Despite its relatively short history, its fortunes were often changing. Periods of rapid growth intermingled with decline and destruction.

Although the first settlements in the area of the present city date back to the 10th century, the original town surrounded with fortifications was built in the second half of the 13th century. The population grew quickly and the town expanded both in its area and meaning. In the 14th century Warsaw was an important town in Mazovia, the province which joined the Polish Crown after the childless death of the last Mazovian duke in 1526. Warsaw obtained the same rights as other towns of the kingdom.

At the turn of the 16th century Warsaw became the capital of Poland. The process took some time. After the great fire at Wawel Castle in Cracow, King Sigismund III Vasa moved to Warsaw Castle in 1596, but he did not settle permanently and together with all his court, until 1611. What decided about Warsaw becoming the state capital were political reasons and the town's convenient situation, closer to the Baltic and Lithuania. A new chapter in the town's history began. Artists, scholars, merchants and craftsmen flew in; magnates built their palaces, as well as churches and monasteries.

The second half of the 17th and early 18th centuries were far from prosperous. The capital was destroyed by successive Swedish invasions and a devastating plague. Under the Saxon kings the town started developing again, but it flourished during the reign of King Stanisław Augustus Poniatowski. Banks and factories were opened, arts and crafts developed, the population increased. The Four-year Sejm, convened in Warsaw in 1788-1792, passed the 3rd May Constitution in 1791.

Towards the end of the 18th century Poland was partitioned among Prussia, Austria and Russia. It took place in three stages: in 1772, 1793 and 1795. Warsaw found itself in the Prussian sector.

After the defeat inflicted on the Prussian army by Napoleon Bonaparte, the Duchy of Warsaw was established in 1807. It did not exist long. The French were soon defeated and in 1813 Warsaw was taken by the Tsarist army. The Congress of Vienna in 1815 brought another change: the

Kingdom of Poland was formed as an autonomous state subordinated to Russia. Unfortunately, the Tsarist authorities violated the constitution, restricted the political freedom of Poles and persecuted the opposition. Clandestine associations were formed and the November Insurrection broke out in 1830. When it fell, the Kingdom lost its whole autonomy. The Citadel became a symbol of the city's subjugation and a silent witness to many executions. Romuald Traugutt, the leader of the January Insurrection of 1863-1864, was executed here, along with other members of the National Government formed by the insurgents.

Poland regained independence after the First World War in 1918 and became the capital of a free country. But as soon as 1 September 1939 the first Nazi bombs fell on the city. The unequal struggle in defence of the city lasted four weeks. During the occupation that followed, the capital again functioned as the centre of underground resistance. Newspapers were published, secret courses were run. The clandestine Union of Armed Struggle gave the beginning to the Home Army. The resistance organization carried out sabotage actions and executions of the most cruel Nazis. The Warsaw Uprising broke out on 1 August 1944. The heroic struggle of Warsaw insurgents and civilians ended in failure. The inhabitants were

displaced from the city and Warsaw was to be annihilated. The Germans blew up and razed to the ground one district after another. They smashed historic relics and monuments of Polish culture, leaving but a sea of rubble.

After the war, Warsaw started to revive quickly. Old inhabitants returned and new settlers arrived. A lot was built, sometimes too hastily and unwisely. The urban shape of the city may now seem chaotic. Huge blocks of flats of prefabricated concrete slabs stand side by side with historic buildings which survived or were reconstructed, and edifices from the period of Socialist Realism neighbour on modern glass constructions. But here the impossible was done: a totally destroyed city was rebuilt within a few years. Historic buildings in the Old Town, Krakowskie Przedmieście and Nowy Świat streets were carefully reconstructed. The Royal Castle was rebuilt. New housing districts, streets and thoroughfares were built. The city is constantly expanding. It acquires more and more skyscrapers, modern office buildings and shopping centres. Old buildings are still reconstructed, like the Town Hall in Teatralny Square. The underground, here called *metro,* is built. Warsaw has every chance to become a truly European metropolis.

View of the Old Town from the Vistula bank.

Sigismund's Column, the first secular monument in Poland, was founded by King Władysław IV to commemorate his father, King Sigismund III Vasa.

The mid-19th-c. fountain in the Saxon Gardens was designed by Henryk Marconi. The Tomb of the Unknown Soldier, seen in the distance, was built inside the preserved fragment of the colonnade of the Saxon Palace, destroyed during the Second World War.

The Prince Józef Poniatowski Monument ornaments the courtyard of the Radziwiłł Palace. Designed by the Danish sculptor Bertel Thorvaldsen, it was founded out of public donations.

The Old Town seen from the Vistula. The green belt along the Vistula escarpment below the Old and New Towns is often a site of various open-air events.

The Monument to Marshal Józef Piłsudski (1867-1935), who fought for Poland's independence as the commander of the I Brigade of the famous Legions. On 11 November 1918 he became head of state and army commander-in-chief. He withdrew from political life in 1923 and returned to it in May 1926, staging a military coup.

The ruins of Warsaw Ghetto. The Germans decided to arrange a Jewish district in October 1940. 450,000 people were crowded behind a three-metre wall. Transports of Jews bound for death camps left from here regularly. In the spring of 1943 an armed uprising broke out in the ghetto, but it was put down with bloodshed, the whole population was murdered and the houses were levelled to the ground.

The Ghetto Heroes Monument was erected at the site of the fiercest fighting. The inscription in three languages - Hebrew, Yiddish and Polish - says: "The Jewish nation to its fighters and martyrs".

Krasińskich Square and part of Długa Street as it looked after the Second World War destruction by the Germans. Next to the severely damaged Piarist Church, the ruins of the monastery, where the Collegium Nobilium, a college for aristocratic boys, was run in 1754-1806.

Krasińskich Square today. The sculptures seen on the photo belong to the 1944 Warsaw Uprising Monument.

The Old Town Market Square. Such view was encountered by the inhabitants who came back home after the liberation. The houses which had not been bombed during the Warsaw Uprising in 1944 were burnt by the Germans after its fall.

The Monument to the Killed and Murdered in the East. one of Warsaw's newest monuments, raised on the traffic island in Muranowska Street near its intersection with Andersa Street.

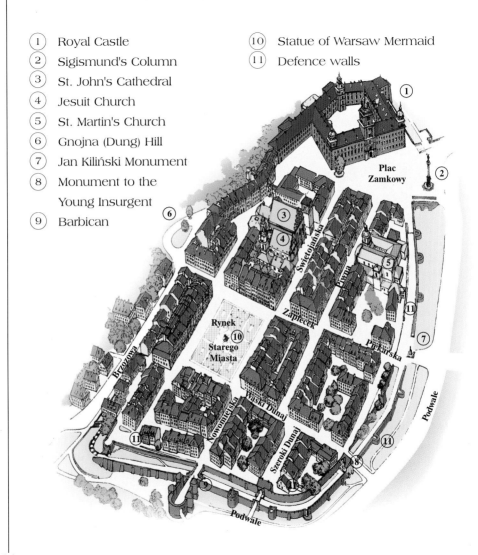

1. Royal Castle
2. Sigismund's Column
3. St. John's Cathedral
4. Jesuit Church
5. St. Martin's Church
6. Gnojna (Dung) Hill
7. Jan Kiliński Monument
8. Monument to the Young Insurgent
9. Barbican
10. Statue of Warsaw Mermaid
11. Defence walls

Plac Zamkowy

Świętojańska

Dunaj

Zapiecek

Rynek Starego Miasta

Piekarska

Brzozowa

Nowomiejska

Wąski Dunaj

Szeroki Dunaj

Podwale

Podwale

THE OLD TOWN AND THE NEW TOWN

The Old Town is one of the most beautiful places in Warsaw. Its romantic streets and corners encourage not only visitors but also the city dwellers themselves to stroll around the place where the history of the city began.

The Royal Castle is a pride of Varsovians. It stands on the site of the original wooden fortress raised at the end of the 13th century by the Mazovian dukes. One of its oldest parts is the Great House, or the Great Court. Its Gothic façade is still visible from the Great Courtyard. The Castle was continuously rebuilt and, like the whole city, it suffered destruction by wars, uprisings and looting. The greatest blow was struck by the Nazis during the Second World War. The Castle was blown up after the fall of the Warsaw Uprising in 1944. Its reconstruction began in 1971. Thirteen years later it was opened for visitors, but the interior decorations are still carried on.

Young people favour the stairs under Sigismund's Column, the oldest secular monument in Poland, built by King Władysław IV in 1644 to commemorate his father, King Sigismund III Vasa.

The reconstruction began soon after the liberation. The original street layout was preserved. Houses and churches were reconstructed according to old prints, photos and even some paintings. Every preserved piece of walls, floors and ornaments was used. Original details of façades, doors or windows were often purposefully left unplastered.

The Market Square has been the focus of life in the city for centuries. It was lined with imposing houses of the richest burghers, such as Fukiers', Basilisk or St. Anne's. In the 15th century a town hall was erected in the middle of the square, but it was pulled down in 1817. Today the Market Square is an eventful place, where music is often played and artists sell their paintings. In summer, cafés fill the square with their tables and colourful parasols; souvenir vendors are seen everywhere. The Historical Museum of the City of Warsaw in the Old Town Market Square is worth visiting in order to see many historic relics connected with the capital.

Religion took an important place in the life of burghers in the past. Each day was subordinated to the rhythm of the church. As thanksgiving and plea for redemption, temples were widely founded by kings and dukes as well as by some of the less wealthy faithful, and various gifts were donated to them. The Old Town has three churches: the oldest St. John the Baptist's in Świętojańska Street, the Jesuit Church close by and St. Martin's in Piwna Street.

The unique atmosphere of the Old Town is created by its charming streets and lanes. Kamienne Schodki, a passage leading down the narrow stairs towards the Vistula, is considered the most beautiful street in Warsaw. In Kanonia, a small triangular square behind the Cathedral, one cannot resist expecting some medieval lady or a thoughtful canon holding a prayer book to appear from the gate any minute.

Initially, the whole Old Town was surrounded by an earthen rampart. At the end of the 14th century defence walls with gates and bastions were built. Although they were partly dismantled in the 18th and 19th centuries, large portions can still be seen, including the fine Barbican, built in 1548 to close the town from the north.

Outside the Barbican, the New Town begins, a remainder of another town called New Warsaw. Its beginning dates to the 14th century, when the people flowing into the town could no longer find a place to live in Old Warsaw and they settled in the neighbourhood. New Warsaw received town rights in 1414. The two separate towns with their own town councils and mayors were not joined until 1792. Houses in the New Town are much more modest than those in the Old Town, but there are fine churches, like the Baroque Church of the Nuns of the Holy Sacrament and the Church of the Visitation of the Holy Virgin Mary in Przyrynek Street.

Castle Square with Sigismund's Column and the Royal Castle façade on the right. The steps of the column pedestal are usually occupied by young people, while the smooth surface around is used for skateboarding and roller-skating. In front of the Castle, Warsaw fiacres wait for passengers.

The Royal Castle stands at the site of the wooden fortress built by the Mazovian dukes in the 13th c. Rebuilt throughout centuries, it became a permanent royal seat in the early 17th c. During the Second World War it was destroyed by the Germans. Carefully reconstructed, it is now the pride of Varsovians and the goal of most visitors to the capital. Above: The Royal Castle Clock, or Sigismund Tower seen from Piwna Street. Right: The Castle seen from the East-West Thoroughfare

The Marble Room, designed by Jakub Fontana, is one of the most beautiful Castle interiors. It was reconstructed according to the water colours by Jan Christian Kamsetzer from 1784. Apart from fine marble finish, the room boasts some saved portraits of Polish kings by Marcello Bacciarelli and sculpted allegories of Peace and Justice by André Le Brun.

◁ The Ballroom (or Great Assembly Hall) in the wing facing the Vistula, built in 1740-46. The room, designed by Domenico Merlini and Jan Christian Kamsetzer, is ornamented with statues of Apollo and Minerva by André Le Brun, saved from war damage.

Knights' Room (or Senator's Anteroom), designed by Jan Christian Kamsetzer, contains six big paintings by Marcello Bacciarelli referring to Polish history and ten portraits of famous Poles by the same artist. Besides, there are marble sculptures of Fame by André Le Brun and Saturn by André Le Brun and Giacomo Monaldi, as well as some bronze busts of famous Poles by the same sculptors.

Horse-drawn Warsaw cabs in the Castle Square. The triangular Castle Square was laid out by the architect Jakub Kubicki at the beginning of the 19th century. Several houses, the Cracow Gate, stables and coach-houses were pulled down to make room for the square. In the mid-19th century the Bernardine Church and convent between the Castle and St. Anne's Church was demolished.

Piwna Street leads from Castle Square to Szeroki Dunaj Street, crossing Zapiecek Street. A walk along Piwna Street offers jeweller's shop windows, the Zapiecek Gallery and a few restaurants.

The Old Town has some enchanting corners, like the passage between Piwna and Świętojańska streets. In the left photo it is seen from Świętojańska Street; the perspective is closed by St. Martin's Church. The other photo shows the same passage from Piwna Street, opening to the façade of St. John's.

A sculpture on one of the Old Town houses. In old towns every house had to differ from others, so they were decorated with sculptures, bas-reliefs or murals, from which the houses took their names.

Świętojańska Street. The first façade on the right belongs to St. John's Cathedral, the oldest of Warsaw churches. It was built as the castle chapel and parish church, became a collegiate church in 1406 and a cathedral in 1798. It was constantly rebuilt and extended. After the last war it was restored to its early-19th-c. shape. Next to it stands the Jesuit Church of Our Lady of Grace, the patron saint of Warsaw. The church, founded by King Sigismund III Vasa, was built in 1608-26.

Kanonia, a small square at the back of the Cathedral, was named after Warsaw canons who lived in nearby houses. It is exceptionally quiet there.

Dawna (Ancient) Street, actually resembling one in an old print, leads to the Vistula escarpment, from where a view extends over the river and right-bank Warsaw, called Praga.

Old Town Market Square. Its four sides were named after people of merit for Warsaw in 1915. The photo shows parts of the north, Dekert side, and the east, Barss side. In summer, cafés fill the square with their tables and colourful parasols and fiacres invite for a ride.

27

The Monument to Jan Kiliński, a shoemaker who led the rising in Warsaw during the Kościuszko Insurrection in 1794. The monument stands opposite Piekarska (Bakers') Street at the former public execution site known as the Little Hell.

The Monument to the Young Insurgent (of 1944), a deeply moving sculpture by Jerzy Jarnuszkiewicz, stands on the defence walls facing Podwale Street. It is always decorated with flowers.

◁ Foollowing removal and renovation, the Mermaid of Warsaw come back to the Old Town Market Square. She had come to symbolise Warsaw by the Middle Ages, appearing on the town's books, documents and seals, and remains the emblem of the capital to this day.

Fragment of the Old Warsaw defence walls, erected at the end of the 14th c. The Barbican on the photo, built in 1548 according to the design by the Italian architect Giovanni Battista of Venice, fortified the Nowomiejska (New Town) Gate, protecting the town from the north.

The Barbican, once fortifying the New Town Gate, today has taken on a different function. Here, street musicians play and artists paint portraits on the spot, fortune is told, amulets and other mysterious objects are sold.

The Baroque Church of the Nuns of the Holy Sacrament in the New Town Market was built in 1688-92 to the design by Tylman van Gameren. Its construction is said to be connected with the vows Queen Marie-Casimire took before her husband John III Sobieski's departure for his campaign against Turks.

◁ St. Jack's Church in Freta Street in the New Town, owned by the Dominican Order, was built in 1603-38, and the nearby monastery in 1638-39. During the Warsaw Uprising the church, turned into a field hospital, was hit by bombs and hundreds of patients died under the rubble.

The Church of the Visitation of the Holy Virgin Mary in Przyrynek Street, the oldest church in the New Town, was founded by Duchess of Mazovia Anna Danuta in 1411.

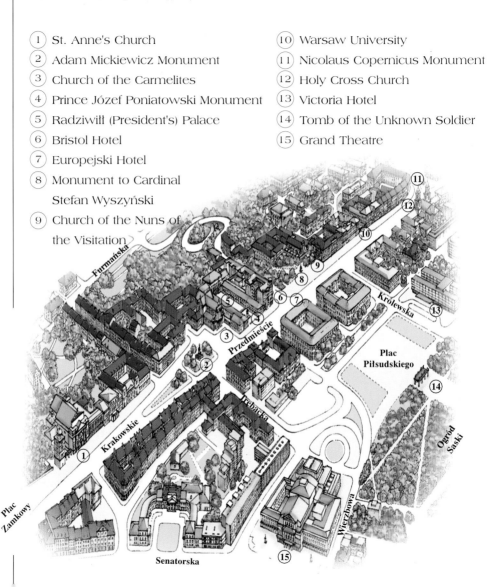

1. St. Anne's Church
2. Adam Mickiewicz Monument
3. Church of the Carmelites
4. Prince Józef Poniatowski Monument
5. Radziwiłł (President's) Palace
6. Bristol Hotel
7. Europejski Hotel
8. Monument to Cardinal
   Stefan Wyszyński
9. Church of the Nuns of
   the Visitation
10. Warsaw University
11. Nicolaus Copernicus Monument
12. Holy Cross Church
13. Victoria Hotel
14. Tomb of the Unknown Soldier
15. Grand Theatre

THE ROYAL WAY

The Royal Way is a line of streets linking Castle Square with Łazienki Park. The route starts in Krakowskie Przedmieście, then goes along Nowy Świat and Aleje Ujazdowskie. It was named so, because the kings used to take this road when travelling to Jazdów, Łazienki, Wilanów and Czersk.

Krakowskie Przedmieście is lined with numerous splendid buildings. Palaces, churches, hotels and beautiful burghers' houses give a special atmosphere to the street. Most of them where built by magnates, who settled in Warsaw in the 17th and 18th centuries.

Here we find the campuses of two institutions of higher education: Warsaw University and the Academy of Fine Arts. Hordes of students fill the street with life.

Four magnificent churches stand in Krakowskie Przedmieście. St. Anne's Church is now an academic church, where students like to be wed. The Gothic walls of the chancel have remained from the initial temple, founded in 1454 by the Mazovian dukes for the Bernardine monks then invited to settle in Poland. In the proximity of the church stands the figure of Our Lady of Passau. The nearby Church of the Carmelites was built at the end of the 17th century and its façade dates from the 18th century. The Baroque Church of the Nuns of the Visitation, exceptionally beautiful when bathed in spring greenery, is thought to be Warsaw's most beautiful temple. Its white and golden interior is captivating, especially the Rococo pulpit in the shape of St. Peter's boat and other precious works of art: e.g. the high altar and the ebony tabernacle from 1654. Next to the church is the Baroque convent. The Holy Cross Church dominates the last section of Krakowskie Przemieście. The sculpture of Christ Carrying the Cross is placed on the top of the stairs. Inside the church rest the urns with the hearts of Frédéric Chopin, brought back from France as the composer had wished, and the writer and Noble Prize winner Władysław Reymont.

Krakowskie Przedmieście and its vicinity boast the greatest number of former residences of magnates, now occupied by state offices. The Radziwiłł Palace is now the seat of the President of the Republic of Poland. On the opposite side of the street, the Potocki Palace houses the Ministry of Culture and Art. The University uses the small but very fine Casimir Palace, as well as the Uruski and Tyszkiewicz palaces. The Academy of Fine Arts owns the late-Baroque Czapski Place. At the end of Krakowskie Przedmieście stands the Staszic Palace, now housing the Polish Academy of Sciences.

The Bristol Hotel, built in the early 20th century and recently renovated, is widely considered as the most beautiful and elegant of Warsaw hotels. It used to be the scene of many political and cultural events.

Several monuments are found in Krakowskie Przedmieście. The Monument to the great poet Adam Mickiewicz stands on a small green square. The equestrian statue of Prince Józef Poniatowski ornaments the courtyard of the Radziwiłł Palace. Near Bristol Hotel stands the monument to the writer pen-named Bolesław Prus, whose novels are mostly set in Warsaw; he is depicted as if he were just taking his usual walk. In front of the church of the Nuns of the Visitation is the Monument to Cardinal Stefan Wyszyński, the primate of the millennium, and in front of the Polish Academy of Sciences - the Monument to the great astronomer Nicolaus Copernicus.

The next section of the Royal Way, Nowy Świat Street, has no such splendid edifices as Krakowskie Przedmieście, but owing to its countless shops, cafés and restaurants, as well as numerous theatres and cinemas in the proximity, the street stays alive till late hours.

The Stock Exchange building at the corner of Nowy Świat and Aleje Jerozolimskie is the former Party House, the headquarters of the Central Committee of the Polish United Workers' Party, for decades the ruling party in post-war Poland. It was built out of obligatory public donations.

Nowy Świat joins Aleje Ujazdowskie in Trzech Krzyży Square, with St. Alexander's Church in the middle. Aleje Ujazdowskie is a fine broad avenue, lined with former aristocratic and bourgeois mansions bathed in the greenery of their parks and gardens. In the 19th century it became the most elegant Warsaw street, where it was in vogue to take a walk or drive in a carriage. After the last war the avenue has maintained its stately atmosphere, enhanced by the presence of many foreign embassies and government buildings. Ujazdowski Park is small but charming.

Ujazdów Castle, rising on the Vistula escarpment near Na Rozdrożu Square, was built as a summer residence for King Sigismund III Vasa. Burnt during the Warsaw Uprising, the castle was pulled down and was not reconstructed until the 1970s. Today it houses the Contemporary Art Centre. On the other side of Agrykola Street spreads Łazienki Park.

View from Castle Square towards Krakowskie Przedmieście Street. On the right, John's House, named after one of its owners, Alexander John. It was reconstructed after the war exactly after a painting by Bernardo Belotto, called Canaletto. Krakowskie Przedmieście is a busy street, with beautiful architecture as well as countless restaurants and cafés.

St. Anne's Church, founded in 1454 by the Mazovian Dukes for the Bernardine monks then invited to settle in Poland. Gothic walls of the chancel have remained from the initial temple. After the Swedish invasion, the church was rebuilt in the Baroque style. In the late 18th c. the Baroque façade was replaced with a neoclassical one. The high altar designed by Tylman van Gameren dates from 1677-80. In the 1740s the interior was decorated with wall-paintings by Brother Walenty Żebrowski. The monastery adjoining the church dates back to 1513.

The Church of the Carmelites, also called St. Mary's Assumption or St. Joseph the Betrothed's, was designed by Giuseppe Belotti and built in the Baroque style at the end of the 17th c. The neoclassical façade was added in 1782.

The Monument to the great poet Adam Mickiewicz was put up out of public donations on the 100th anniversary of his birth. The pedestal bears the inscription: "To Adam Mickiewicz · Compatriots".

Fragment of Krakowskie Przedmieście with the early 18th-c. Rococo Wessel Palace at the corner of Kozia and Trębacka streets. Initially it housed the Saxon Post Office. Later rebuilt, it became an apartment house. Reconstructed after the war, it houses the regional public prosecutor's offices. Close by in Kozia Street resides the Museum of Caricature.

The Radziwiłł Palace. The main part of the palace was built in the first half of the 17th c. In the 18th c. side wings were added. In the period of the Kingdom of Poland, the Tsarist Governor resided in the palace from 1818. It was then remodelled into a neoclassical building. When Poland regained independence in 1918, the palace became the seat of the prime minister. During the Second World War it was occupied by the Germans. After the war, it housed the Council of Ministers until 1994, when it became the residence of the Polish president. The upper photo shows the palace seen from the gardens. Right, the Prince Józef Poniatowski Monument in the palace courtyard.

The Baroque Church of the Nuns of the Visitation was built in the first half of the 18th c. As it was never destroyed by wars, the original interior decoration has been preserved. In front of the church stands the Monument to Cardinal Stefan Wyszyński, the Primate of Poland.

The Bristol Hotel, completed in 1901, became famous for its great balls and parties, including the celebration of Maria Skłodowska-Curie's Nobel Prize or the singer Lucyna Messal's success on stage. Jan Kiepura sang to the crowds of his fans from the hotel balcony.

The University of Warsaw area is entered through the neo-Baroque main gate designed by Stefan Szyller in 1900. Opposite the gate is the main library. The University, opened in 1816, was formed of two earlier existing schools: the Collegium Medicus and the College of Law and Administration. It has survived till these days despite repression by consecutive occupiers. The campus has a unique atmosphere, created by students.

The clock on the main library (BUW), built in the neo-Renaissance style in 1891-99. The building is now too small to contain the ever-enlarged book collection of a modern university. Soon the majority of them will be transferred to the modern building under construction in the Powiśle district.

The Casimir Palace, the oldest university building, was erected at the initiative of King Władysław IV in 1634 and in 1660 it became a summer residence of kings John Casimir and then John III Sobieski. It housed the Knights' College in 1765-68. The next rebuilding was carried out in 1815-17, for the University. Today the palace, reconstructed after the last war, houses the rector's office and the University museum.

◁ The Baroque Holy Cross Church was erected in 1682-96 along with the monastery buildings. The façade and two towers were added later. In the mid-19th c. the sculpture of Christ Carrying the Cross was placed on the top of the stairs.

The Nicolaus Copernicus Monument, designed by the Danish artist Bertel Thorvaldsen, stands in front of the Staszic Palace, belonging to the Polish Academy of Sciences. The pedestal bears the inscription in Latin and Polish: "To Nicolaus Copernicus Compatriots".

The palace and park complex of the Academy of Fine Arts. The statue in front of the palace is a copy of the Venetian monument by Andrea Verocchio dating back to 1488 and depicting a condotiere named Bartolomeo Colleoni.

The Ostrogski, also called Gniński Palace, in Tamka Street, leading down the escarpment towards the Vistula. It has a long history and its owners changed many times. Today it is the seat of the Frédéric Chopin Society and the museum of the composer. The building is connected with the legend about the Golden Duck.

Nowy Świat Street, a part of the Royal Way, is lined with luxury shops and stores as well as cafés. The street itself is a fine show of all styles in fashion and beauty. Wide pavements encourage to walk and elegant shop windows to do some shopping.

St. Alexander's Church in Trzech Krzyży Square, where Nowy Świat Street joins Aleje Ujazdowskie (Ujazdów Avenue), was built in 1818-26 according to the design by Christian Piotr Aigner, modelled on the Roman Pantheon. The church was remodelled and enlarged at the end of the 19th c. After the last war, it was reconstructed in its original form.

The Sheraton Hotel in Trzech Krzyży Square is one of the youngest Warsaw constructions, quite successfully designed to suit the neighbouring architecture.

Agrykola

Ogród
Botaniczny

Promenada

Al. Ujazdowskie

Belwederska

Droga Chińska

Gagarina

1. Palace on the Water
2. Myślewicki Palace
3. Museum of Hunting
4. Great Annex
5. Old Guardhouse
6. Monument to King John III Sobieski
7. Theatre on the Island
8. New Orangery
9. Egyptian Temple
10. Belvedere
11. Temple of Diana
12. Frédéric Chopin Monument
13. Józef Piłsudski Monument
14. Water Container
15. White Cottage
16. New Guardhouse
17. Old Orangery

The magnificent 18th-century palace-cum-garden complex attracts crowds of visitors and Warsaw inhabitants in every season of the year. Łazienki Park is a favourite place for a walk on a nice holiday.

It was developed at the site of the medieval hunting forest of the Mazovian dukes residing at Jazdów. In the second half of the 17th century Grand Marshal of the Crown Stanisław Lubomirski, then the owner of Jazdów, built two small pavilions in the forest: the Hermitage and the Bath, both designed by Tylman van Gameren. The domed circular hall of the Bath imitated a grotto with a fountain in the middle and the bathroom was supplied with two tubs. That was the origin of the name Łazienki, in Polish 'baths'.

In 1764 Ujazdów Castle and its environs were bought by King Stanisław Augustus Poniatowski, who intended to adapt Łazienki for his summer residence. In order to make the Bath suitable for living, it had to be enlarged and refurbished. As a result, a beautiful Palace on the Water was built, also called the Palace on the Island. Some other buildings were also erected and the park was arranged.

One of the finest additions, the Myślewicki Palace, was built for Prince Józef Poniatowski. The first building erected in Łazienki for King Stanisław Augustus was the White Cottage designed by Domenico Merlini. It is a small house with all sides identical. Here the monarch stayed when the Palace on the Water was under construction. The Old Orangery, one of the largest buildings in the park, was provided with big windows for the cultivation of tropical plants. One of the two wings was and still is a theatre, with interior decoration all made of wood. It was for many years directed by Wojciech Bogusławski, the founder of the Polish national theatre at the end of the 18th century. The New Orangery houses a restaurant. The Great Annex, built initially to house the servants and the palace kitchen, later accommodated the famous Cadet School.

The round building opposite the Old Orangery is the Water Container, from which water used to flow along wooden pipes to the palaces.

The park owes its romantic character to picturesque alleys and bridges as well as to the structures modelled on ancient architecture: the Temple of

Diana, the Egyptian Temple and the Theatre on the Island, with an island stage decorated with an imitation of ruins of the ancient Temple of Jove in Baalbek.

In summer the sound of music is heard throughout the park. When piano concerts are held at the Frédéric Chopin Monument, it is hard to find a free seat on nearby benches.

Łazienki Park adjoins the Warsaw University Botanical Gardens, founded in 1818 on Łazienki grounds. It contains some 8000 species of plants, including trees, shrubs and flowers, both local (e.g. a 200-year-old oak) and exotic. It is especially attractive in springtime, with all the colours of blooming flowers. Within the garden area stands the Astronomical Observatory and still remain the foundations for the Temple of Providence, founded by King Stanisław Augustus to celebrate the 3rd May Constitution but never erected.

The early-18th-century Belvedere Palace is situated on the top of the escarpment, facing Belwederska Street. The name derives from the Italian belle vedere, meaning a "fine view", which is exactly what it offers. The palace was always strictly connected with the history of Warsaw. King Stanisław Augustus Poniatowski bought it to accommodate his court. He also set up a royal faience factory in its annex. From 1818 separated from the Łazienki area, the palace was rebuilt into the residence of Tsarist viceroys. Between the two world wars Marshal Józef Piłsudski resided in the palace. Towards the end of the Second World War the Germans intended to blow it up, as it is shown by holes for explosives they bored in the walls. Fortunately, they never managed to fulfil their plan. After the liberation the Belvedere Palace remained a state building, until 1994 the seat of the president of the Republic of Poland.

The Palace on the Water was the summer residence of King Stanislaw Augustus Poniatowski, extended from the former Bath of Prince Lubomirski. The sculptures on the terrace in front of the palace include Satyr dancing with a bacchante and Hermaphroditus with a nymph by André Le Brun, as well as personifications of the Vistula and Bug rivers by Ludwik Kauffmann. The terrace itself is the most frequented spot in Łazienki.

The Theatre on the Island for 1500 viewers was designed by Jan Christian Kamsetzer. The summer theatre still in use first opened on the anniversary of Stanisław Augustus's election, 7 September 1791, with the ballet performance Cleopatra.

Łazienki Park with the Palace on the Water in the distance. In summer you may have a romantic trip by boat on the pond and see the magnificent nature around, with rare species of trees and shrubs.

The Monument to King John III Sobieski on the stone bridge over the pond was designed by André Le Brun. It was unveiled on 14 September 1788, on the 105th anniversary of the king's victory over the Turks at Vienna.

The Old Orangery was built in 1786-88. Apart from tropical plants, it houses the permanent exposition of plaster-of-Paris and marble sculptures, some of which have remained from King Stanisław Augustus' collection. A terrace decorated with flowers spreads in front of the building.

The New Orangery, built in 1860, houses a tropical garden ornamented with sculptures and the Belvedere restaurant. ▷

The Belvedere Palace is now outside the Łazienki area. Although no longer the seat of the president of the Republic of Poland, it continues to be used for stately occasions, such as visits of heads of state, who often reside here.

The Monument to Frédéric Chopin in Łazienki Park. The first bronze sculpture was put up in 1926. During the last war it was cut up by the Germans into pieces and sent to a metal works. It was reconstructed and returned to its original site amid flower-beds in 1958.

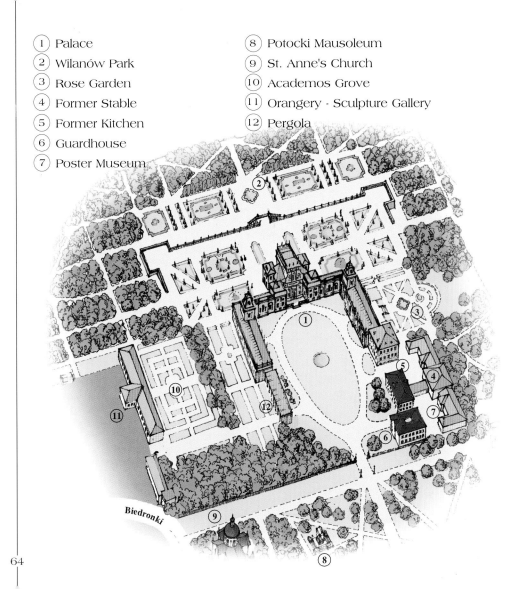

1. Palace
2. Wilanów Park
3. Rose Garden
4. Former Stable
5. Former Kitchen
6. Guardhouse
7. Poster Museum
8. Potocki Mausoleum
9. St. Anne's Church
10. Academos Grove
11. Orangery - Sculpture Gallery
12. Pergola

Biedronki

WILANÓW

The 17th-century residence of King John III Sobieski lies in the south of Warsaw. The king purchased the village of Milanowo with a view to building his summer palace there. Built in stages from 1677 till 1696, it was first called Villa Nuova. Initially a low manor-house with four corner extensions, later it was added a mezzanine and two galleries with towers, and finally a full storey in the central part. Enriched with ornaments, it looked like a Baroque villa. The residence was intended to be the monument of King Sobieski's glory. The monarch was glorified by sculptural decorations which depicted him at his victorious battles, especially his victory over the Turks at Vienna. Figures of ancient heroes symbolized the king's virtues. Also representations of his spouse, Marie-Casimire, popularly called Marysieńka, fill a lot of decorative space. The queen's virtues, such as beauty, wisdom, loyalty and fertility, are personified by Greek goddesses in sculptural form.

In the following centuries the palace owners kept changing and they made further extensions. Side wings were added and some other buildings erected. The estate stayed the longest, i.e.

nearly for a hundred years, in the hands of the Potocki family. In the late 19th century it was bequeathed to the Branickis, who owned it until 1945. At the end of the last war the Germans seized the palace for a hospital and barracks. They devastated the buildings, the park and its facilities, and upon leaving, they took away almost all valuables. After the liberation, Wilanów was declared state property and a branch of the National Museum was established in the palace. A greater part of the collections have been regained. Today the royal and magnates' rooms from the 17th, 18th and 19th centuries are open to visitors, as well as the Polish Personalities Painting Gallery from the 16th through 19th centuries, the largest in the country. Several hundred paintings show not only the faces of famous celebrities, but also the change in fashions, hair styles and painting techniques throughout the centuries. Concerts are staged on the palace terrace in summer.

One of the Wilanów owners was Stanisław Kostka Potocki, an outstanding personality of the Polish Enlightenment: a statesman and deputy to the Great Sejm, a man of broad education and author, a great art admirer and collector. He built the neo-Gothic gallery in the north wing, where the first museum was opened for the public in 1805. The visitors were greeted by the Latin inscription on the floor, meaning "free entrance to everyone". The credit for the largest part of the present art collection in Wilanów goes to Potocki.

The palace is surrounded by a wonderful park. The oldest part, extending between the palace and the lake, is a two-level Italian garden with a terrace. The balustrades of the upper garden and the stairs are decorated with mid-18th-century sculptures. South of the palace is the Romantic English-Chinese park arranged by Princess Izabela Lubomirska, with a stone column to the memory of Ignacy and Stanisław Potocki and a sarcophagus for the latter. A Romantic landscape park with an artificial island on the lake stretches north of the palace. The Monument to the Battle of Raszyn fought against Austrians in 1809 stands on the island, which is connected with the shore by the Roman Bridge. Nearby is the Chinese Summer-house.

Apart from the beautiful palace and gardens, at Wilanów one finds a gallery of decorative arts in the former orangery and the Poster Museum. The building of the museum is an interesting combination of the old with the new architecture: a modern pavilion was added to the old façade of the riding school which survived the war.

The Church of St. Anne in the park area dates from 1772. Nearby is the neo-Gothic mausoleum of Stanisław Kostka and Aleksandra Potocki.

Wilanów is the most beautiful Baroque palatial residence within the borders of Warsaw and one of the finest in Poland. It is sometimes called "Little Versailles".

The bridge and main gate lead to the palace courtyard, where another epoch is entered. One of the most beautiful magnates' residences in Poland was built owing to King John III Sobieski's aversion to the noisy city and his love of country life, as well as to the massive investments of consecutive owners.

The Wilanów Palace front side. The palace is richly ornamented with sculptures, stucco and paintings, most of which refer to King John III and glorify his brevity and wisdom as well as the virtues of his whole family. The supraporta with a sibyl on the wall of a corner extension shown on the photo is an exceptionally fine piece of decoration.

◁ The south wing of the palace facing the gardens; the small rose garden was laid out in the mid-19th c. A fountain with the sculpture of a putto with a swan stands in the middle of the flower carpet.

The garden side of the main part of the palace. On the photo, the two-level garden in Italian and French style, arranged by Adolf Boy in 1682, in King Sobieski's time.

Fragment of the Italian-French garden between the palace and the Wilanów lake. The garden has a geometric design of lawns, decorative flower parterres and lush bushes. It is ornamented with fountains, sculptures and fabulous trimmed hedges.

◁ The neoclassical Orangery, which acquired its present form in 1806-21, houses a decorative art gallery. The garden in front of the Orangery is called the Academos Grove.

A fountain in the Wilanów gardens. The park is charming in any season, but it reaches its full beauty in spring and summer, when its vast greenery is brightened by thousand-coloured flowers.

73

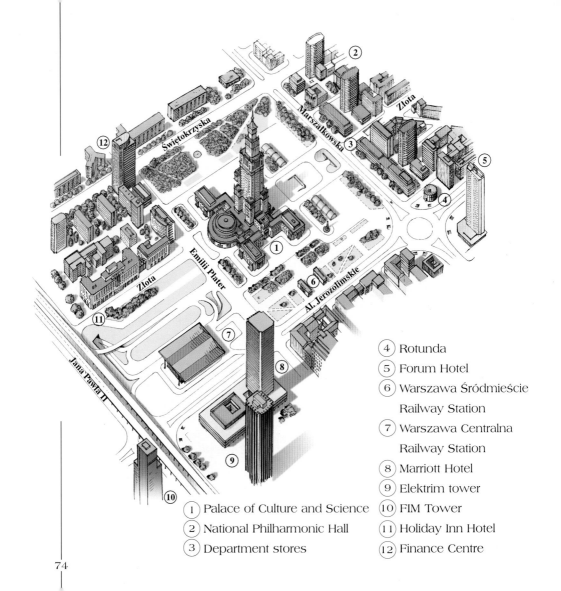

4 Rotunda
5 Forum Hotel
6 Warszawa Śródmieście
 Railway Station
7 Warszawa Centralna
 Railway Station
8 Marriott Hotel
9 Elektrim tower
10 FIM Tower
11 Holiday Inn Hotel
12 Finance Centre

1 Palace of Culture and Science
2 National Philharmonic Hall
3 Department stores

THE CITY CENTRE

In the past, a market square constituted the city centre. It usually had a town hall in the middle, surrounded by shops and stalls always crowded with townspeople. They not only did shopping, but also met other people, gossiped and heard important municipal and royal announcements. An old market square was a sort of the press, radio and television combined. Warsaw was no exception. But as the town grew, the actual city centre shifted away from the old market square. The modern centre of Warsaw is completely different from the historic one.

Most tours coming to Warsaw start their sightseeing from the Palace of Culture and Science, whose terrace on the 30th floor offers a fine panorama of Warsaw. A gift from the USSR nations, the structure, which became one of Warsaw's most controversial hallmarks, was built in the years 1952-1955 in the central spot of the city to replace the houses destroyed during the last war. It is 234 metres high including the spire and houses numerous institutions, such as cinemas, theatres and museums, restaurants and shops. There is the Palace of Youth cultural centre and the huge Congress Hall. Many events are held in the Palace, including book, computer, pharmaceutical, medical equipment and other fairs.

Many plans of the Palace demolition, conversion or surrounding it with high-rise buildings have been conceived, but there are also many voices for leaving it as it is, or just... cleaning it a bit. The square in front of the Palace has temporarily been turned into a building site of the underground (metro) station.

Aleje Jerozolimskie opposite the Palace is lined with some beautiful turn-of-the-century buildings characteristic of Warsaw Art Nouveau style. A curiosity in one of these houses is the still working peep-show from the beginning of this century.

The City Centre directly reflects the changes that have occurred in recent years. New office buildings, shops and hotels spring up, either in the form of modern glass constructions or adjusted to the old environment. Some reconstruction of historic buildings is still being made. It seems nearly everyone drives a car these days. The streets are clogged and so are all possible (and impossible) parking spaces.

Warsaw City Centre is an agglomeration not only of offices and shops, but also of cinemas, theatres and museums. There is the Philharmonic Hall, the Opera House and the Operetta. The imposing building of the Warsaw University of Technology was erected in 1899-1900 out of public donations. Its main, pentagonal building has a huge main hall in the middle, covered by a glass roof and encircled by galleries. The west side of Bankowy Square is worthy of note, with its neoclassical palaces designed by Antonio Corazzi and built in 1823-1830: the former seat of the government commission for revenue and the ministry of treasury house the present City Hall and other municipal authorities; the former stock exchange building has been turned into a museum.

The nearby Saxon Gardens was the first Warsaw park, open to the public in 1727. Behind the park, in Józefa Piłsudskiego Square is the Tomb of the Unknown Soldier, built to commemorate the soldiers who died in the First World War. The remains of a soldier killed in combat near Lvov and 14 urns with the earth from battlegrounds were symbolically buried in the tomb. After the Second World War, urns with the earth from its battlegrounds were added. The ever-burning fire is guarded by soldiers.

On one side of Piłsudskiego Square stands the Zachęta building, now the Central Bureau of Art Exhibitions, always offering some interesting exhibition. On the other side looms the back wall of the Grand Theatre and Opera House built by Antonio Corazzi in 1825-1833 and raised from ruins after the last war. The most outstanding opera and ballet masters performed on this stage.

Warsaw is becoming more and more colourful, not only for the brave colours of plaster on house walls, but also for the overflow of billboards and ads on trams and buses. They have already been accepted as putting a bit of colour to everyday life in the city.

The centre of Warsaw as viewed from Chałubińskiego Street. A blend of styles and epochs has created a unique character of the city. Trends in architecture keep changing fast: skyscrapers have sprouted up amid older buildings like in any big city.

The Palace of Culture and Science dominates its close vicinity. Built after the Second World War in the early 1950s, it has quite unexpectedly become a tourist attraction of contemporary Warsaw, especially that it offers a fine panorama of the whole city from the terrace on the 30th floor.

Warsaw by night. The Congress Hall, seating 3200, is a part of the Palace of Culture and Science. Numerous cultural events, such as concerts and recitals, as well as official meetings, rallies and conferences are held here.

Marszałkowska Street. From the left, a department store, the bank rotunda and the Forum Hotel built in 1972-73 by a Swedish company as one of the first high-rise buildings in Warsaw. The reconstructed rotunda was blown up by gas explosion in February 1979 killing 49 people. The monument to the victims stands nearby.

Defilad (Parade) Square used to be the site of military parades and public meetings. Most recently it has served as an open market. On the opposite side of Marszalkowska Street, the complex of department stores, high-rise apartment and office blocks, a cinema and the bank rotunda, all connected by a pedestrian mall with many small shops and cafés, built in 1961-68, is known as the East Wall.

81

The Holiday Inn Hotel, one of the newest Warsaw hotels, in Złota Street near the Centralny railway station.

The turn-of-the-century buildings in Aleje Jerozolimskie show the influence of various then trendy styles in architecture, such as Art Nouveau or historicism.

The city centre viewed from the Holiday Inn Hotel: the Centralny railway station, built in 1972-75; behind it the Marriott Hotel with LOT ticket offices and expensive shops inside; on the right the newly built FIM Tower. The street is called Aleja Jana Pawła II (John Paul II Avenue).

The city centre by night. The brightly lit youngest of Warsaw railway stations, Warszawa Centralna, can serve 150 thousand passengers and 30 trains per hour. On the right, the lower storeys of the Marriott Hotel.

Atrium, the modern office and shopping centre, ▷ widely considered as one of the finest recent constructions in Warsaw, forms a part of the huge complex to be raised on the west side of Aleja Jana Pawła II.

Rondo ONZ (UNO Roundabout) with the ▷
new office tower above it. The cityscape of
Warsaw keeps changing rapidly. With new
buildings mushrooming everywhere, for
some rare comers the Śródmieście district
may look unrecognizable.

The Mercure Hotel, a modern hotel built
a few years ago in Aleja Jana Pawła II. The
local confectioner's offers excellent French
cakes.

All Saints' Church in Grzybowski Square.

Konstytucji (Constitution) Square is a part of the MDM (Marszalkowska Residential Quarter) extending from Wilcza Street to Zbawiciela Square. It was built in 1950-52 and included the modernization of some houses that survived the war. Numerous shops, cafés and restaurants occupy the lower storeys.

The Warsaw University of Technology main building was designed by Stefan Szyller and erected at the close of the 19th c. Sculptures by Pius Weloński and Zygmunt Langman ornament the façade. The huge main hall in the middle is covered by a glass roof and encircled by galleries. The initial Polytechnic School, founded by Stanislaw Staszic in 1825, was closed twice in times of the partitions of Poland: after the November Insurrection in 1831 and after the student strike in 1905. Reopened as the Warsaw University of Technology in 1915, it has since been active except during the Second World War.

The City Hall of Warsaw resides in the horseshoe-shaped former palace of the government commission for revenue, one of the so-called Treasure Palaces on the west side of Bankowy Square, designed by Antonio Corazzi and built in 1823-30. They were rebuilt after the war destruction in the 1950s.

The modern "Blue Skyscraper" rising in Bankowy Square opposite the City Hall houses banks, offices and a number of shops.

The Grand Theatre. Its imposing building was designed by Antonio Corazzi, who incorporated the preserved fragment of the earlier structure. The construction started in 1825 and the first performance was staged eight years later. The theatre burnt in 1939. During the post-war reconstruction, the old façade was preserved. The Grand Theatre has the biggest operatic stage in Europe and the auditorium seating 1900. The most outstanding opera and ballet masters from all over the world have performed here.

The Jablonowski Palace next to the Blank Palace opposite the Grand Theatre is a recent reconstruction, made to suit the surroundings. Its façade is an exact copy of the pre-war palace, which used to house the Warsaw Town Hall.

The Tomb of the Unknown Soldier was built in 1925 inside the colonnade of the Saxon Palace. The palace was partly blown up during the Second World War, but the Tomb together with a fragment of the colonnade survived. It is now a symbolic monument, containing the remains of a soldier killed in combat, urns with the earth from battlegrounds and slabs with names of places where Polish soldiers fought in both world wars. In front of the Tomb, state celebrations are held, official delegations and common people lay flowers to pay homage to those who died for freedom.

Marshal Józef Piłsudski Square. On the left a fragment of the Victoria Hotel, built in 1974-76. Close by in the small Małachowskiego Square, the Zachęta gallery, dating from 1903, where contemporary Polish and foreign art exhibitions are held. The huge dome belongs to the adjoining Protestant Church.